SATISFYING
● = INTERNAL CUSTOMERS
FIRST!

A Practical Guide To
Improving Internal And External
Customer Satisfaction

Richard Y. Chang

P. Keith Kelly

Jossey-Bass
Pfeiffer
San Francisco

RICHARD
CHANG
ASSOCIATES

Copyright © 1994 by Richard Chang Associates, Inc.

ISBN: 0-7879-5082-3

Published by

350 Sansome Street, 5th Floor
San Francisco, California 94104-1342
(415) 433-1740; Fax (415) 433-0499
(800) 274-4434; Fax (800) 569-0443

www.pfeiffer.com

Printing   10   9   8   7   6   5   4   3   2   1

ACKNOWLEDGMENTS

About The Authors

Richard Y. Chang is President and CEO of Richard Chang Associates, Inc., a diversified organizational improvement consulting firm based in Irvine, California. He is internationally recognized for his management strategy, quality improvement, organization development, customer satisfaction, and human resource development expertise.

P. Keith Kelly, a Senior Consultant at Richard Chang Associates, Inc., is an experienced educator, consultant, and management professional. His special areas of expertise encompass strategic planning and analysis, financial management, process improvement, and market research.

The authors would like to acknowledge the support of the entire team of professionals at Richard Chang Associates, Inc. for their contribution to the guidebook development process. In addition, special thanks are extended to the many client organizations who have helped us shape the practical ideas and proven methods shared in this guidebook.

Additional Credits

Reviewers:	David W. Crouch, Jim Greeley, and Christina Slater
Editor:	Sarah Ortlieb Fraser
Graphic Layout:	Christina Slater
Cover Design:	John Odam Design Associates

PREFACE

The 1990's have already presented individuals and organizations with some very difficult challenges to face and overcome. So who will have the advantage as we move toward the year 2000 and beyond?

The advantage will belong to those with a commitment to continuous learning. Whether on an individual basis or as an entire organization, one key ingredient to building a continuous learning environment is *The Practical Guidebook Collection* brought to you by the Publications Division of Richard Chang Associates, Inc.

After understanding the future *"learning needs"* expressed by our clients and other potential customers, we are pleased to publish *The Practical Guidebook Collection*. These guidebooks are designed to provide you with proven, *"real-world"* tips, tools, and techniques— on a wide range of subjects—that you can apply in the workplace and/or on a personal level immediately.

Once you've had a chance to benefit from *The Practical Guidebook Collection*, please share your feedback with us. We've included a brief *Evaluation and Feedback Form* at the end of the guidebook that you can fax to us.

With your feedback, we can continuously improve the resources we are providing through the Publications Division of Richard Chang Associates, Inc.

Wishing you successful reading,

Richard Y. Chang
President and CEO
Richard Chang Associates, Inc.

TABLE OF CONTENTS

1. **Introduction** 1
   Why Read This Guidebook?
   Who Should Read This Guidebook?
   When and How To Use It

2. **Customer Satisfaction From The Inside Out** 5
   Satisfying Internal Customers
   Customer Feedback
   Customer Loyalty
   The Cost Of A Dissatisfied Customer

3. **Improving Internal Customer Satisfaction—A Model** 13
   Case Example: ZampleCo

4. **Step One: Measure External Customer Satisfaction** 23
   Why Measure It?
   What To Measure?
   How To Measure It?
   Focus Groups

5. **Step Two: Map The Internal Chain** 41
   Map Successive Layers Of The Internal Chain
   Map A Detailed Chain From External Suppliers To External Customers
   Map Based On The Organizational Structure

6. **Step Three: Locate The Critical Links** 51
   Measure All The Links In The Chain
   Measure From The Outside In
   Have The External Customer Pinpoint The Critical Links

7. **Step Four: Analyze The Critical Links** **61**
   Internal Customer Satisfaction Questionnaire
   Internal Chain Of Events Flow Chart
   Cause And Effect Diagram

8. **Step Five: Resolve Critical Link Issues** **75**
   Establish Who Should Be Involved
   Decide What Should Be Done
   Resolve The Issues According To Plan

9. **Step Six: Evaluate Changes** **85**
   Why Evaluate?
   Starting Over From The Top

10. **Summary** **91**

Appendix: Reference Materials **93**
   Sample Internal Customer Questionnaire
   Tips For Defining Internal Customer Requirements
   Developing A Flow Chart

> "Consumption is the sole end and purpose of all production; and the interests of the producer ought to be attended to, only so far as it may be necessary for promoting that of the consumer."
>
> *Adam Smith*
> 1776

CHAPTER ONE

INTRODUCTION

Customer loyalty and satisfaction are becoming more difficult and more important to maintain in today's competitive business world. Keeping your customers satisfied is the key to ensuring they come back. And making sure they keep coming back is, as we will see, vitally important to the bottom line.

Customer satisfaction doesn't only apply to the end user of your organization's products or services; it also applies to the people in your organization, and how they work together to produce products and services.

Why Read This Guidebook?

This book provides a road map to improve customer satisfaction, with both your external and internal customers. The same principles that apply to keeping external customers happy apply to keeping internal customers happy, too.

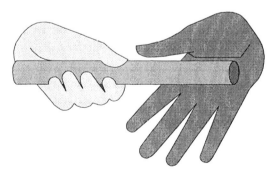

So, what's an internal customer? Think about a track-and-field relay team. When one runner passes the baton to a teammate, they are engaging in internal customer interaction. Both runners are part of the same team, yet the second runner's ability to run a good race and make a successful hand-off to the next member of the relay team depends on how smoothly the first runner passes the baton (*thus satisfying his or her internal customer*). These relationships affect not only the next leg of the race, but the success of the entire team.

If your team wants to win the race against your competitors, you need to work to make sure that your hand-offs are smooth and effective. As you can see, internal relationships have a profound impact on your organization's ability to run a good race and to provide your customers with the kind of service that will keep them coming back for more.

This guidebook presents specific tools for measuring and increasing customer satisfaction. Think of it as a blueprint to achieve external customer satisfaction and loyalty.

Who Should Read This Guidebook?

This guidebook provides valuable concepts and tools for you to use, whether you are a manager, team leader, team member, salesperson, engineer, or quality professional. The approaches presented in the following chapters are adaptable to a service or manufacturing setting, as well as profit or nonprofit organizations, both large and small.

When And How To Use It

Unfortunately, many companies wait until problems are full-blown before they concern themselves with customer satisfaction. By then, it is often too late. Focus on customer satisfaction long before the loyalty of your customers ever comes into question.

Organizations spend a lot of time tracking customer satisfaction. Unfortunately, the employees responsible for tracking satisfaction are not always those responsible for making the necessary changes to increase satisfaction. This guidebook's easy-to-read, step-by-step format and practical tools help you and your team go beyond merely tracking to actually improving customer satisfaction.

Let's take a closer look at the dynamics involved in creating external customer loyalty by satisfying internal customers first!

CUSTOMER SATISFACTION
FROM THE INSIDE OUT

On an external level, there is a Supplier-Producer-Customer relationship between organizations and a final customer. For example, Company A supplies materials, services, or information to Company B, which incorporates those inputs into a new package of goods or services for Company C, the end user *(or customer)*.

Supplier   Producer   Customer

Satisfying Internal Customers

Gaining and keeping customer loyalty through customer-satisfaction efforts starts with activities along your organization's internal chain of events.

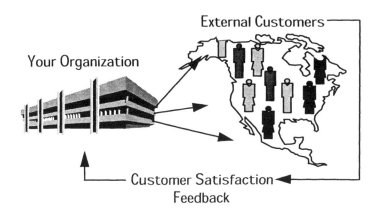

External Customers

Your Organization

Customer Satisfaction
Feedback

Each of these internal events, or processes, overlap each other at the hand-off points between internal customers, producers, and suppliers. These overlap points, shown here as the intersection points of the circles, form links in a chain. Each link represents a point where internal customer satisfaction can be tracked and improved.

The goal of any customer-satisfaction effort should be to improve external satisfaction levels by first improving internal customer relationships.

One of the key ingredients for determining and managing customer satisfaction, both inside and outside the organization, is feedback.

Customer Feedback

Customer feedback speaks in many voices from a whisper to a shout. If you haven't set up a system of communication with your customers, you may not have a means of recognizing and interpreting the warning signs of low satisfaction levels. Instead you may see the end results, such as: reduced sales, high rates of customer turnover, and so on. Low satisfaction levels end up costing your organization money in two ways:

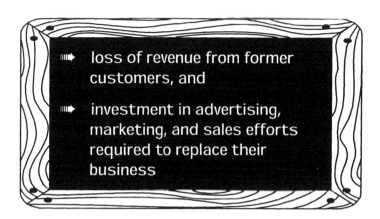

loud→ loss of revenue from former customers, and

loud→ investment in advertising, marketing, and sales efforts required to replace their business

While you could consider these signs a type of customer feedback, they aren't exactly the type of feedback that's best for your organization. To maintain customer satisfaction, you must manage the customer feedback loop.

Customer Loyalty

Vital to creating and maintaining customer loyalty is the knowledge needed to capture that seemingly elusive prey.

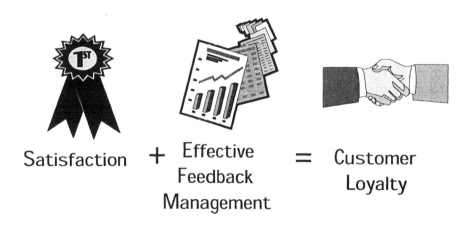

Satisfaction + Effective Feedback Management = Customer Loyalty

Customer loyalty is the result of satisfaction and effective feedback management inside and outside of the organization. It is more than just a concept—it can be measured in dollars and cents.

The Cost Of A Dissatisfied Customer

Making customer satisfaction a premium would be important if it only affected the revenue end of your organization's scale. It is significantly important when you realize that a lapse in customer satisfaction can cost you more than lost business.

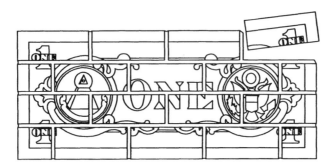

In the following example, a set of calculations shows the costs of replacing dissatisfied customers.

Company X has an annual revenue of $1 million. An estimated $50,000 is budgeted for marketing to replace customers lost to the competition. Company X's current customer base includes 400 clients, 75 percent of whom are loyal and 25 percent of whom are fence sitters. Eighty percent of the fence sitters are likely to switch to another supplier at a moment's notice—because they are not satisfied.

For Company X, the losses total 80 customers. Divide the marketing budget by the number of lost customers, and the replacement cost per customer equals $625. The cost of replacing lost customers added to the amount of revenue lost to the competition, results in a costly situation. Clearly, there are bottom line advantages to maintaining customer loyalty by actively ensuring customer satisfaction.

THE COST OF CUSTOMER DISSATISFACTION—COMPANY X

A. Annual revenue	$1 million
B. Marketing budget to attract new customers because of customer turnover	$50,000
C. Number of current customers	400
D. Percentage of loyal customers	75%
E. Number of loyal customers (C x D)	300
F. Number of customers considered fence sitters (C - E)	100
G. Percentage of fence sitters who become dissatisfied during the year	80%
H. Number of lost customers (G x F)	80
I. Cost of replacing each lost customer (B ÷ H)	$625

Customer feedback, satisfaction, and bottom-line results like those above can all be managed by focusing on internal customer satisfaction first!

CHAPTER TWO WORKSHEET: SATISFYING YOUR CUSTOMERS

1. Calculate the costs of replacing lost customers.

   A. Annual revenue $ _____

   B. Marketing budget to attract new customers $ _____

   C. Number of current customers _____

   D. Percentage of loyal customers _____ %

   E. Number of loyal customers (C x D) _____

   F. Number of customers considered fence sitters (C - E) _____

   G. Percentage of dissatisfied fence sitters _____ %

   H. Number of lost customers (G x F) _____

   I. Cost of replacing each lost customer $ _____

2. What issues have been raised in your organization regarding customer satisfaction and its implications?

   _____

   _____

   _____

   _____

   _____

   _____

3. What efforts have been made to improve or encourage customer satisfaction in the past six months?

_____

_____

_____

_____

_____

_____

_____

_____

4. What have the results been?

_____

_____

_____

_____

_____

IMPROVING INTERNAL CUSTOMER SATISFACTION—A MODEL

It is of little value to know that customer satisfaction levels need improvement if you don't have the tools to improve them.

This six-step model directs you and your team toward the fulfillment of your goals. It begins with measuring external customer satisfaction and ends with measuring the results of your actions.

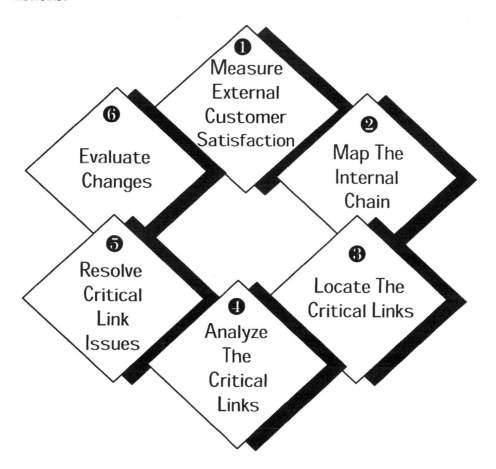

Let's look at an overview of the six steps leading to success.

Step 1: Measure external customer satisfaction

As any carpenter knows, there's a sound reason for the adage, *"measure twice, cut once."* Carpenters recheck their measurements, because if they act on a questionable measurement, they waste time and valuable materials. With customers, if action is taken on a hunch, a small problem easily becomes a larger one. Measure customer satisfaction before you take further action.

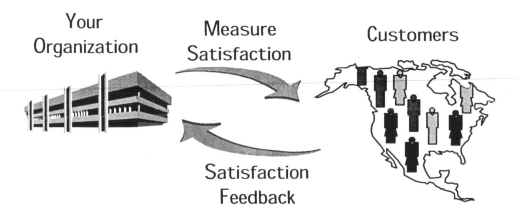

Within this first step are four key substeps:

    A. Identify your customers' requirement areas

    B. Determine your surveying methodology

    C. Develop survey/interview questions

    D. Survey/interview your customers

Step 2: Map the internal chain

Just like a relay team, your team relies on a series of hand-off relationships. The smoothness of these relationships affects your group's success in delivering what your external customers want. Mapping out hand-off relationships, and specifying who passes what off to whom, creates a powerful, customer-oriented atmosphere in your organization.

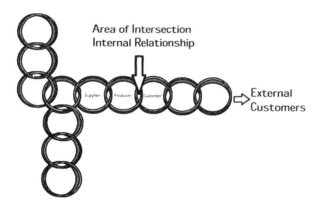

Step 3: Locate the critical links

Deciding the relationships that are crucial to external customer satisfaction is vital for improving customer satisfaction. We'll look at the three valuable tools determining the critical links you should improve.

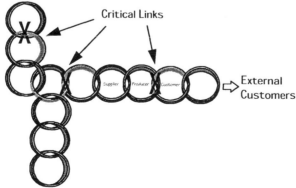

Step 4: Analyze the critical links

Knowing that a person is ill does very little in helping a doctor to make a diagnosis. At this stage of the process, learn valuable techniques to separate symptoms from problems, and focus on important issues at the critical links.

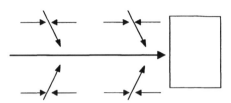

Step 5:   Resolve critical link issues

Here you will learn skills and techniques helpful for you and your team to make changes to improve the quality of your internal chain of relationships and to improve your output as an organization.

Work Flow Tasks	Responsibility	Accountability	Accountability
Select sheets	Anthony, Byron	Pete (Assembly)	Angela (Assembly)
Check sheets for adequate cool down	Anthony, Byron	Pete (Assembly)	Angela (Assembly)
Measure and mark drill holes	Richard, Byron	Pete (Assembly)	Angela (Assembly)

Step 6:   Evaluate changes

Evaluating your changes and their results justifies the time, effort, and money going into making satisfaction-oriented changes.

ZampleCo is a organization that uses recyclable tin . .

.

to manufacture filing cabinets. The company has been growing slowly but steadily for nearly 10 years. When the company was founded, it was the only one of its kind. ZampleCo enjoyed a kind of celebrity status, gaining a lot of free press because of its creativity in making a practical product out of recycled materials.

Lately though, others have copied ZampleCo's product, starting similar companies in different parts of the country. Although ZampleCo's sales haven't been affected much by the new competitors, the management team decided to be proactive and *"head them off at the pass."*

After much discussion at a recent management meeting, Marvin, one of the three co-owners, summed up the approach when he said, *"Up to this point, our customers bought from us because we were the only game in town, not necessarily because they were loyal ZampleCo customers. The rules of the game have changed. From here on in, we'll succeed as a company only if we have loyal and satisfied customers. Our first challenge is to find out if they are satisfied, and if not, to do something about it."*

One of the managers responded with, *"Yes, you're right, and the idea of satisfied customers is something we can apply within the company, too. After all, if there is something we're doing inside the company that is contributing to customer dissatisfaction, it would surely come to the surface if we were to look at internal customer relationships, too."*

"Good point," replied Marvin. *"If we solve any internal customer satisfaction issues, we improve external customer satisfaction at the same time."*

Marvin agreed to lead a team made up of Brenda, the manager of Assembly; George, one of the senior sales representatives; and Julio, one of the staff from the Material Production division. They agreed that their mission was to improve overall customer satisfaction by looking at internal and external customers.

CHAPTER THREE WORKSHEET:
THE STEPS TO SATISFIED CUSTOMERS

Perhaps some recent experiences in dealing with customer satisfaction issues came to mind as you were reading this chapter. Or perhaps you were thinking ahead to how you might adapt or apply the steps in your organization. Here's your chance.

1. Step 1: Measure external customer satisfaction

    a. What has been done in your organization in the past two years to measure external customer satisfaction?

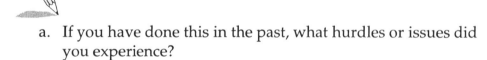

_____

_____

_____

2. Step 2: Map the internal chain

    a. If you have done this in the past, what hurdles or issues did you experience?

_____

_____

_____

    b. What issues might you experience in the future?

_____

_____

_____

c. How might you overcome those issues if they arise?

_____

_____

_____

3. Step 3: Locate the critical links

   a. What issues have you experienced inside your organization when focusing on improving customer satisfaction?

   _____

   _____

   b. What issues will you experience in the future?

   _____

   _____

   c. How will you overcome these issues if they arise?

   _____

   _____

4. Step 4: Analyze the critical links

   a. What tools or methods have you used in the past to analyze causes of customer satisfaction issues?

   _____

   _____

   _____

b. What have your successes been in these situations?

_____

_____

_____

_____

c. What have your challenges been in these situations?

_____

_____

_____

_____

5. Step 5: Resolve critical link issues

a. What have been the keys to your successes in the past?

_____

_____

_____

_____

b. What pitfalls have you encountered at this phase?

_____

_____

_____

_____

c. What might you do differently in the future?

_____

_____

_____

_____

_____

6. Step 6: Evaluate changes

a. What benefits do you see in doing this?

_____

_____

_____

_____

_____

b. What challenges do you foresee?

_____

_____

_____

_____

_____

STEP ONE: MEASURE EXTERNAL CUSTOMER SATISFACTION

Why Measure It?

Why is it important to measure how satisfied your customers are? Have you ever kept a running mental tally of how satisfied you are with a local pizza restaurant? Have you ever decided to buy pizza from one business and not another, because of your impressions about the taste, quality, or price of the pizzas?

Wouldn't it be useful if these pizza places knew why they were, or were not, getting the business of people like yourself? Likewise, since the customers who use your products or services are running a mental tally of how satisfied they are with your organization's output, wouldn't it be a good idea to establish a method for finding out what their thoughts are, then use this information to increase satisfaction levels?

What To Measure?

Customer satisfaction is a result of your product or service meeting a certain set of customer requirements.

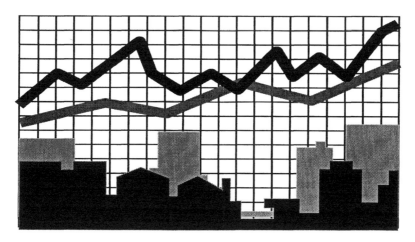

Some of the ingredients that make up this set of customer requirements include:

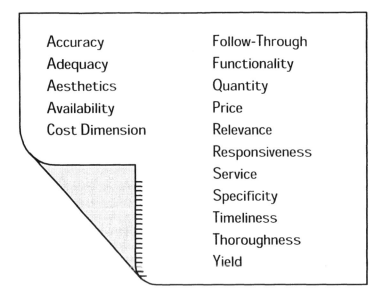

Accuracy	Follow-Through
Adequacy	Functionality
Aesthetics	Quantity
Availability	Price
Cost Dimension	Relevance
	Responsiveness
	Service
	Specificity
	Timeliness
	Thoroughness
	Yield

Since satisfaction results from customers getting what they want, measuring current satisfaction or dissatisfaction levels will yield information about what it is they want but aren't getting. By looking at how to measure customer satisfaction, we will also see how to determine external customer requirements for loyalty.

How To Measure It?

There are several measurement tools you can use with relative ease. They include:

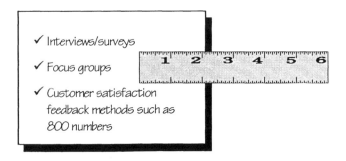

- ✓ Interviews/surveys
- ✓ Focus groups
- ✓ Customer satisfaction feedback methods such as 800 numbers

Interviews/Surveys

Surveys allow you to zero in on specific issues. If you want to know whether or not your external customers are satisfied with shipping practices, then you can write interview/survey questions that pertain to delivery.

Here are four substeps you can take to develop useful interviews and surveys:

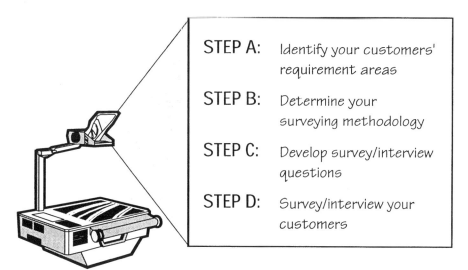

STEP A: Identify your customers' requirement areas

STEP B: Determine your surveying methodology

STEP C: Develop survey/interview questions

STEP D: Survey/interview your customers

Step A: Identify your customers' requirement areas

Why is it important to know your customers' requirement areas before you even design a questionnaire or survey? Because if you don't ask the right questions, it won't matter what the answers are—you still won't find out whether customers are satisfied with the issues that are important to them.

Possible ways to identify customer requirement areas include:

➠ Discussing the issue with a sample group of customers.

➠ Presenting a question to them such as, *"If we were to develop a questionnaire to measure our customers' satisfaction with our organization, what questions should we be asking?"*

➠ Brainstorming with a variety of people within your organization. Since individuals and departments have different customer relationships and perspectives on customer needs, a cross section of ideas will be presented to create a complete picture.

Marvin and each member of his team . . .

agreed to talk to two ZampleCo customers to learn their requirement areas. About half of the contacts were made by phone and the other half were face-to-face meetings. Team members asked each customer the same question:

"What are the key areas you feel ZampleCo should cover when asking our customers how they feel about our products?"

The following week the group got back together and compared notes. Although some of the responses had been more specific than others, the team members realized the issues were not very different. Their fact-finding mission determined that customers were concerned with three main areas:

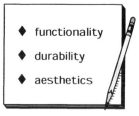

- ◆ functionality
- ◆ durability
- ◆ aesthetics

"It's a good thing we did this first, or we might have made up a questionnaire on issues of billing, speedy delivery, and other things that don't to seem to concern customers," Brenda said.

The group thought it was ready to question the remaining customers to find out how satisfied they were in each of these areas. But George, who had been involved in customer surveys before, said, *"Hold on, we have to figure out the best way to do this first. The way we measure customer satisfaction has to work for the customers and give us the information we need. . . ."*

Step B: Determine your surveying methodology

You will need to make decisions concerning:

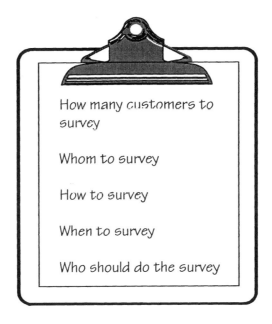

How many customers to survey

Whom to survey

How to survey

When to survey

Who should do the survey

These decisions will determine which questions you ask and how you will ask them. Take a moment and look at the issues before developing the actual questions.

How many customers to survey

The basic rule behind sample selection is to choose a cross section of customers that represent your overall customer base. For example, if one-third of your customers are large companies, one-third are medium-sized firms, and the remaining third are small companies, your sample group should reflect this profile.

Other criteria for selecting the make-up of the sample group might include: percentage of frequent versus infrequent buyers, industry sector, and geographic area.

Note: You may have to make a trade-off, however, between trying to mirror your customer base precisely and breaking your sample group into too many subgroups.

For example, if small companies in industry X are 5 percent of your base, and you are going to survey 50 customers, you would only have two or three respondents in this group. Although they should be in the sample, be careful about interpreting their responses as valid indicators of all small companies in industry X.

Whom to survey

Don't bias your sample. Everyone wants to hear good things from their customers; and, of course, nobody wants to hear from dissatisfied customers. There is a natural tendency to include the positive customer feedback in the sample and to exclude negative feedback. But does this really give you a true picture of how your organization is perceived in terms of customer satisfaction? You need to hear both the good and bad news if you are truly interested in improving customer satisfaction.

How to survey

There are several options, each with its own advantages and limitations. The best method will depend on your situation, how many customers are in your sample group, and what works best for your customers. Highlights of some of these options follow.

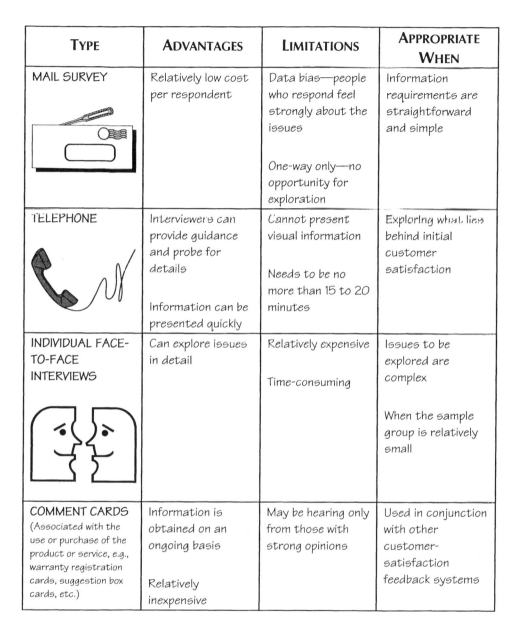

TYPE	ADVANTAGES	LIMITATIONS	APPROPRIATE WHEN
MAIL SURVEY	Relatively low cost per respondent	Data bias—people who respond feel strongly about the issues One-way only—no opportunity for exploration	Information requirements are straightforward and simple
TELEPHONE	Interviewers can provide guidance and probe for details Information can be presented quickly	Cannot present visual information Needs to be no more than 15 to 20 minutes	Exploring what lies behind initial customer satisfaction
INDIVIDUAL FACE-TO-FACE INTERVIEWS	Can explore issues in detail	Relatively expensive Time-consuming	Issues to be explored are complex When the sample group is relatively small
COMMENT CARDS (Associated with the use or purchase of the product or service, e.g., warranty registration cards, suggestion box cards, etc.)	Information is obtained on an ongoing basis Relatively inexpensive	May be hearing only from those with strong opinions	Used in conjunction with other customer-satisfaction feedback systems

Many organizations use different customer satisfaction research methods at the same time, instead of relying on a single measure. Measuring customer satisfaction is one area where it is difficult to argue against the maxim that *"more is better."*

When to survey

Some considerations include:

⟹ The timing issue for your customers (their busy season, time of the month, etc.)

⟹ When you need the information for internal decisions (timing of product enhancements, advertising and marketing campaigns, etc.)

⟹ When you can do something tangible and visible with the information (the process of gathering customer-satisfaction information creates expectations that you will do something visible with it in a reasonable amount of time)

Who should conduct the interviews/surveys

Hundreds of marketing research firms provide excellent information and service. Several advantages to having a third party involved in the process include:

➡ They will probably be more objective in formulating questions and analyzing responses

➡ Customers may be more open when providing information to a third party

➡ Professional research organizations have the expertise and the facilities to ensure the process is productive and effective

➡ Alternatively, university and community college business schools often have market research students seeking customer satisfaction projects as part of their course requirements.

However, organizations with long-term commitments in managing customer satisfaction feedback often handle the entire process to ensure continuity, control, and flexibility.

Thanks to the warranty registration cards . . .

that ZampleCo had started using four years ago, the organization had the names and addresses of 900 buyers, even though more than half had bought from office supply stores and other distributors, rather than directly from ZampleCo.

The team interviewed half of this group via a mailed questionnaire. A random sample was selected by a simple method. Every second name was chosen from the list of buyers who had sent in cards.

Several repeat buyers reduced the list to 400 names. The process was repeated until 450 names were chosen.

As the team went through the list of names, Julio suggested setting up the questionnaire in a way that would divide the responses into three groups. This would allow the team to compare levels of satisfaction and determine how these levels affected sales.

GROUP 1: Customers who have purchased more than once (including a purchase in the last year)

GROUP 2: Customers who have purchased more than once, but have not purchased in the last year

GROUP 3: Customers who have only purchased once

"Good idea," replied Brenda. *"Can everyone get together next Monday so we can put the questionnaire together? . . ."*

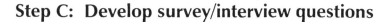
Step C: Develop survey/interview questions

Interview your internal or external customers with a short list of open-ended questions inviting free responses, or specific questions requiring forced-choice answers *(such as a numeric scale),* or a combination. The appropriate tool for the interview/survey method chosen has one objective in mind—providing feedback on customer requirements.

When the information is gathered through face-to-face interviews, a predetermined set of questions are used for the following reasons:

✓ To keep the interviews on track

✓ To ensure consistency in responses from one interview to another

✓ To let your customer know that you are thorough and organized when gathering customer-satisfaction information

Here's a look at a draft of ZampleCo's questionnaire.

QUESTIONNAIRE

KEY: **1** = strongly disagree, **2** = disagree, **3** = neither agree nor disagree, **4** = agree, and **5** = strongly agree.

1.	The drawers on ZampleCo cabinets slide freely	**1**	**2**	**3**	**4**	**5**
2.	The latches work well	**1**	**2**	**3**	**4**	**5**
3.	The locks always work well	**1**	**2**	**3**	**4**	**5**
4.	Drawers are easy to open and close	**1**	**2**	**3**	**4**	**5**
5.	ZampleCo cabinets are designed well	**1**	**2**	**3**	**4**	**5**
6.	The cabinets are more than strong enough to meet my needs	**1**	**2**	**3**	**4**	**5**
7.	The cabinets' drawers and hardware hold up well with frequent use	**1**	**2**	**3**	**4**	**5**
8.	The cabinets' physical appearances blend well into office surroundings	**1**	**2**	**3**	**4**	**5**
9.	The cabinets retain their physical appearance over time	**1**	**2**	**3**	**4**	**5**
10.	ZampleCo cabinets provide good value for the price	**1**	**2**	**3**	**4**	**5**
11.	The cabinets come well packaged to prevent damage	**1**	**2**	**3**	**4**	**5**
12.	Overall, I am very satisfied with ZampleCo cabinets	**1**	**2**	**3**	**4**	**5**

Martin, George, Brenda, and Julio . . .

spent more than two hours working on a questionnaire to test customer satisfaction regarding functionality, durability, and aesthetics. After testing the questionnaire on colleagues *(and making minor revisions)*, they decided to add questions to cover other areas of internal concern primarily the issues of price, and whether the packing boxes were adequate to prevent damage to the cabinets up to the time customers unpacked them . . . .

Step D: Survey/interview your customers

Customers appreciate being asked for their feedback, and have come to expect it in some industries. Whichever method you use to gather information, do it in a way that shows the customers you sincerely desire their feedback and are serious about using their input. Thank each respondent for his or her participation.

The team decided that ZampleCo employees . . .

would conduct the survey. This allowed them to let their customers know the organization was sincerely interested in their feedback. The team recruited colleagues to stuff 450 envelopes with questionnaires to be mailed by the targeted date. ZampleCo offered a $5 donation to the charity of the respondent's choice for each completed questionnaire.

Three weeks later, the results of the questionnaire were tallied. Customers were satisfied with ZampleCo's products, with the exception of the functionality and durability of the cabinet locks and the latching mechanism.

Based on the scoring method in the questionnaire, the team calculated overall customer satisfaction at 76 on a scale of 1 to 100. Everyone agreed this score allowed room for improvement . . . .

Note: In many cases the feedback from external customers will not be this specific. Companies often measure satisfaction on an ongoing basis using an index *(such as a scale of 1 to 100)*. When the numbers dip, a organization needs to look carefully at its internal customer satisfaction to pinpoint critical links, or trouble spots.

Focus Groups

Focus groups are structured group interviews designed to gather feedback through two-way interaction between participants. Focus groups are often used to explore issues of a survey or interview, and uncover the reasons behind the issues.

	ADVANTAGES	LIMITATIONS	APPROPRIATE WHEN
FOCUS GROUPS	Can observe body language, tone of voice, etc. Interaction between participants can provide insight that may not otherwise come up	Limited to subjects that can be handled comfortably in a group setting—may not be appropriate if your customers are competitors	You want ideas for designing a customer satisfaction survey/question-naire You want to explore a specific issue in depth

Unless you have conducted or observed focus groups, strongly consider using a professional focus group facilitator. He or she will structure the focus group session, prepare a group interview guide, and run the session, making sure specific customer satisfaction information is obtained.

Martin and the group decided . . .
that conducting a focus group would be a good way to gather customer feedback on changes made to the cabinets based on the customer satisfaction survey.

CHAPTER FOUR WORKSHEET:
MEASURE EXTERNAL CUSTOMER SATISFACTION

1. What are your organizations' specific reasons, or objectives, for measuring customer satisfaction?

_____

_____

_____

2. How would these objectives be communicated? To whom?

_____

_____

_____

3. How will you determine customer requirement areas?

_____

_____

_____

4. Your survey methodology:

a. How many customers will you survey?

_____

_____

b. Which customers will be included in the survey?

_____

_____

_____

c. Which surveying techniques will you use?

_____

_____

_____

d. When will the interviews/survey take place?

_____

_____

_____

e. Who will conduct them?

_____

_____

_____

_____

5. How will you design a questionnaire or list of questions?

_____

_____

_____

_____

6. Who needs to be involved?

_____

_____

_____

_____

_____

7. What questions will you ask? (**Hint:** _Identify the answers you need first, and then write questions to give you those answers.)_

_____

_____

_____

_____

_____

8. How will you test the questionnaire?

_____

_____

_____

_____

_____

STEP TWO: MAP THE INTERNAL CHAIN

From the time your organization starts producing its product or service to the time you deliver it to your external consumer, the product or service being changed for consumption goes through an internal chain of events.

In that chain, everybody is a customer, a producer, and a supplier. When you accept the baton from a teammate, you are a customer. When you run with it for your leg of the relay, you are a producer—making some change or adding value to the baton. When you pass it off to the next member of the team, you become a supplier.

If you identify the chain of events in your organization and note where internal customer relationships exist, you can increase your definition of customer requirements for each link in the chain, setting the stage to identify links where difficulties have developed, and make changes at those critical links.

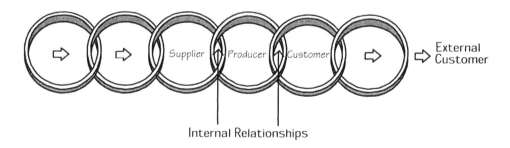

Supplier | Producer | Customer | External Customer

Internal Relationships

The chain of internal relationships is represented visually in a format we'll refer to as a map. The map shows major work processes as circles, and the relationship between these processes *(between customers, producers, and suppliers)* as the areas where the circles intersect.

Three possible approaches to creating this map include:

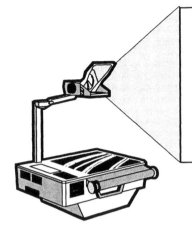

A. Map successive layers of the internal chain

B. Map a detailed chain from external suppliers to external customers

C. Map based on the organizational structure

Let's take a brief look at these methods, their advantages, limitations, and appropriate use.

A. Map Successive Layers Of The Internal Chain

This approach involves creating a *"big picture"* chain first, showing the major steps. More detailed maps follow until the level of desired detail is reached.

Following is an example of the first two layers of internal maps for ABC Mortgage Company.

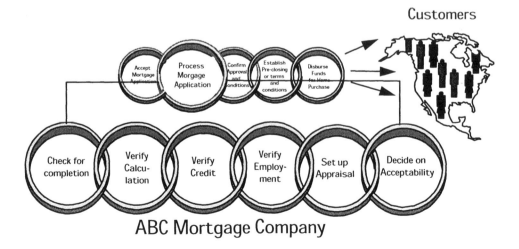

Advantages of this method:

➠ It looks at the core of the organization's business, focusing on the basics of what is being done for the customer.

➠ It identifies the largest issues first, saving time and effort by avoiding repeatedly solving the same problem at lower levels.

Disadvantages of this method:

➠ Dealing with an issue at a high level that might be solved easily at a lower level.

➠ Lower-level employees with hands-on exposure and valuable insight might be left out of the early stages of the mapping.

This method is applicable when:

➠ You want to force your team to look at issues concerning the whole organization rather than focusing on one area.

➠ You want to include people from different parts of the organization in the process, allowing each one to contribute ideas based on his/her role in the successive layers of the map.

B. Map A Detailed Chain From External Suppliers To External Customers

This method starts with the external customer and creates a single detailed map, without the benefit of layers. The map resembles a wiring diagram for a computer, with hundreds of links in the chain.

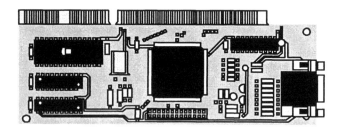

Advantages of this method:

➡ It is thorough.

➡ It forces you to look at things the organization does that might not otherwise be evident. For example, an organization might have certain policies and procedures that were put in place in the past, but are now outdated.

Disadvantages of this method:

➡ It can be very time-consuming. Many people need to be consulted. If they have different opinions about the map, you will have to go back and revise it.

➡ It can become obsolete soon after it is created.

This method is applicable when:

➡ The organization is relatively small.

➡ You are only going to map a section of the overall organization.

C. Map Based On The Organizational Structure

The starting point for the mapping process is the organizational chart. One section of it can be selected for mapping in more detail, or separate maps can be created for different areas at the same time.

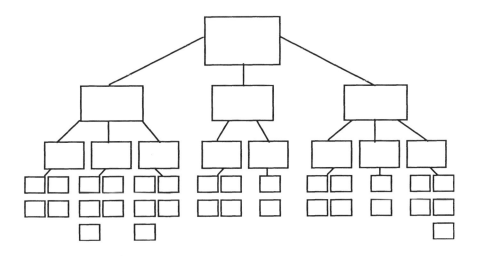

Advantages of this method:

➡ Creating a map is easy when it's based on an existing organizational chart.

➡ You can create a map quickly by using job descriptions and department responsibilities that are already written.

Disadvantages of this method:

➠ Focus is on departments and the current structure rather than the work flow between internal suppliers, producers, and customers.

➠ Turf battles may erupt as departments and groups define their maps in their own terms.

This method is applicable when:

➠ The difference between the organizational chart and the way work flows in the organization is minimal.

Creating such a map does not have to be a time-consuming project. Keep in mind the purpose is to pinpoint areas that connect external customer satisfaction with the critical links in the internal chain. Although the following example is for a small organization with only two levels in its map, creating one for a larger organization with, say, three or four levels, will not be difficult.

Note: Work directly with the people involved in the internal relationships to create detailed levels of your map.

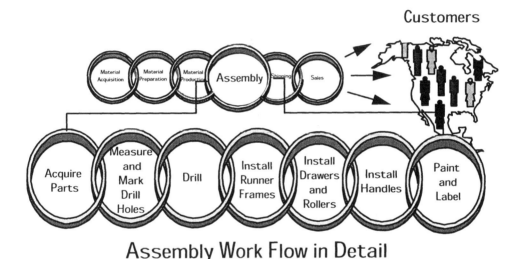

Assembly Work Flow in Detail

Each link in the chain represents a point where decisions are made about the organization's processes. An activity at any one of the links can have a far-reaching effect on your final customers. Because of this, it is important to have a map of the entire chain.

ZampleCo has six departments, . . .

with a handful of people per department. Its Materials
Acquisition department procures the reusable sources of tin.
After it has found the tin, the Materials Preparation department
takes over: cleaning the tin, melting it, and then rolling the
recycled tin into sheets of different thicknesses and sizes for
filing cabinet parts.

After the tin sheets are created, the Material Production
department creates cabinet shells and drawers. Components
such as drawer handles, runners, etc., are purchased from other
manufacturers. The assembly department then puts the
components together as one of three sizes of cabinets. The
cabinets are then sent to the shipping warehouse, which
responds to orders coming in from the sales team—the external
customer contact point.

CHAPTER FIVE WORKSHEET:
MAPPING YOUR INTERNAL CHAIN

1. Which mapping method will you use:

Map successive layers of the internal chain

Map a detailed chain from external suppliers to external customers

Map based on the organizational structure

2. Why did you choose that method?

_____

_____

_____

_____

_____

3. What potential challenges do you foresee in creating your map?

_____

_____

_____

_____

_____

_____

STEP THREE: LOCATE THE CRITICAL LINKS

Critical links are specific points where the causes of external customer satisfaction issues occur. After mapping the chain of internal events, determine where the critical links are.

The approach you choose will depend on whether you are trying to implement an internal customer service climate or pinpoint a specific internal customer satisfaction issue.

The three possible approaches are:

A. Measure all the links in the chain, then select the one with the lowest level of satisfaction—the critical link.

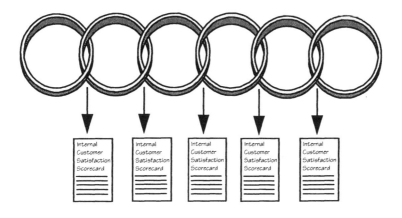

B. Measure from the outside in. Work back from the measure of external customer satisfaction through each link in the internal chain.

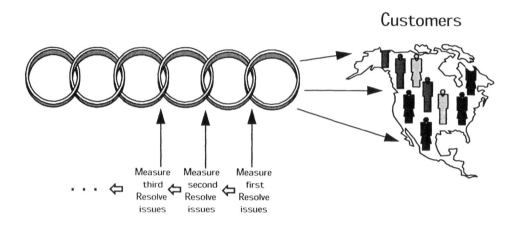

C. Have the customer pinpoint the critical links.

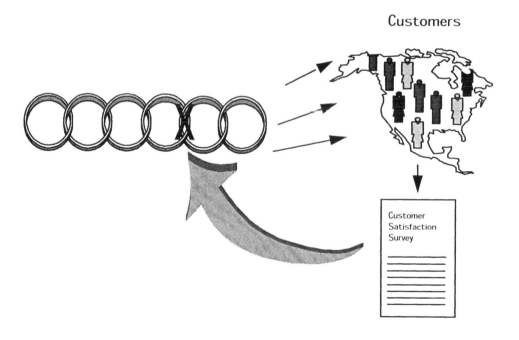

A. Measure All The Links In The Chain

To implement this tool, one person in the team surveys customers and suppliers at each internal link, or distributes questionnaires to everyone in the chain.

Note: In the appendix, you will find a sample survey that you can adapt and use in interviews.

This survey yields an internal customer satisfaction score for each link in the chain. Looking at the scores, determine the average ratings *(a base line)* and see which scores fall below it.

The advantages of this approach are:

➠ By evaluating every link in the chain, you get an overall picture of how well your company's internal customer satisfaction climate is functioning.

➠ If there is more than one trouble spot, they will all be detected.

➠ No one department or group feels singled out.

There are also some disadvantages:

➠ It can be time-consuming, expensive, and disruptive.

➠ It may not lead to the true critical link—the one that is important to the customer.

➠ It can lead to several issues being put on the table at once, increasing the chances of bickering, and a possible stalemate over what to do first.

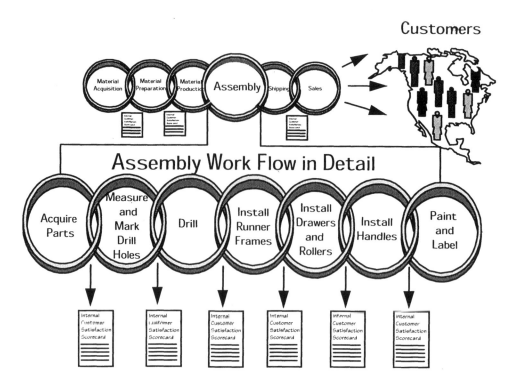

ZampleCo decided to . . .

make internal customer satisfaction an integral part of their corporate culture and climate. Bob, the quality manager, was given the task of assessing the levels of satisfaction for each internal customer relationship. With questionnaires in hand, Bob interviewed representatives of each department at ZampleCo.

While reviewing the satisfaction level scores in his office, Bob noticed that the scores were relatively consistent, except for a dip between Material Production and Assembly. It seemed that Assembly didn't feel it was getting necessary materials from Production. Having located this weak link in an otherwise strong chain, Bob was fairly certain this was the critical link where internal customer satisfaction should be addressed . . . .

B. Measure From The Outside In

This approach views each link in your organization's internal chain of relationships starting from the last link—the external customer. Move from the end of the chain towards the beginning, until you locate the first glitch. After locating a weak link indicating low internal satisfaction levels, deal with it appropriately. Then take another step back in the direction of your external suppliers.

Advantages of this approach include:

⫸ Thorough assessment of the internal satisfaction environment

⫸ The opportunity to learn from and build on each success as you improve internal customer satisfaction at successive links in the chain

Disadvantages of this approach include:

⫸ It is more costly and time-consuming because of stopping and dealing with each link before moving on to the next

⫸ Immediate external customer satisfaction issues may not be addressed soon enough for your customers, since the approach follows the chain of relationships instead of dealing with the links that are critical to the external customer

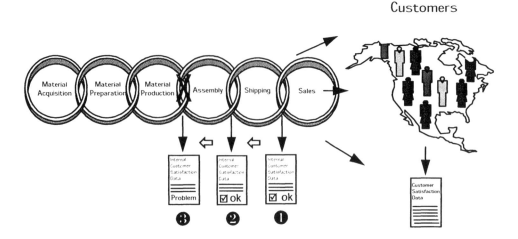

If he used this approach, . . .

Bob would start at the end of the internal chain and work backward. Using his evaluative tools, Bob would first measure how satisfied Sales was in terms of having its requirements met by Shipping. He would then move back to the link between Assembly and Shipping, and so on. Eventually, he would come across the dissatisfaction that existed in the Material Production/Assembly link, and suggest necessary changes there . . . .

C. Have The External Customer Pinpoint The Critical Links

Surveying external customer satisfaction provides clues to your critical link. After you have gleaned information from your customer survey, go to the critical link specified by the customer and implement necessary changes.

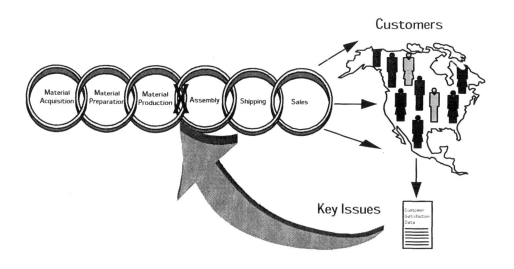

Customers

Key Issues

For example, . . .

if a ZampleCo customer interview revealed a long lag time between placing an order and receiving it, the most obvious link to look at is the one between Sales and Shipping. Any number of variables might contribute to this weak hand-off. Once the link is discovered and dealt with, the results are immediately apparent to the customer, and lag time between ordering and receiving a shipment decreases.

Once you have found the critical link, implement necessary changes, thereby improving satisfaction levels in that relationship. Any changes affect the satisfaction levels throughout the rest of the chain.

CHAPTER SIX WORKSHEET:
LOCATING THE CRITICAL LINKS

1. Which method will you use to locate the critical links?

☐ Measure ali the links in the chain

☐ Measure from the outside in

☐ Have the customer pinpoint the critical links

2. Why did you choose that method?

_____

_____

_____

_____

_____

3. What potential challenges do you foresee in locating your critical links?

_____

_____

_____

_____

_____

4. Who will be involved in the process of pinpointing your
organization's critical links?

_____

_____

_____

_____

_____

_____

_____

_____

_____

_____

_____

_____

_____

STEP FOUR: ANALYZE THE CRITICAL LINKS

After you have located the critical link, determine the nature of the problem and its true causes. In medicine, proper diagnosis and treatment begins with a list of symptoms. To make sure the treatment is thorough, a doctor then determines what is behind the symptoms. This same in-depth diagnosis is necessary to improve the well-being of an organization too, if it is to succeed at delivering customer satisfaction.

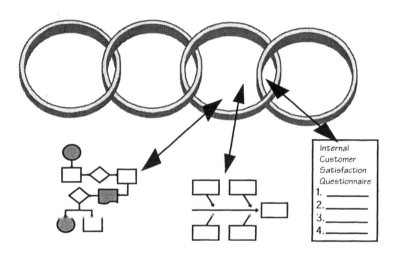

Tools to analyze the critical links

To determine the root causes of problems arising at a critical link, we have provided you with a set of tools for separating the causes of a problem from its symptoms. These tools include the Internal Customer Satisfaction Questionnaire, Internal Chain of Events Flow Chart, and Cause and Effect Diagram.

TOOL	WHERE IS IT USED IN THE CHAIN	ITS ROLE
INTERNAL CUSTOMER SATISFACTION QUESTIONNAIRE Questionnaire	At the linkage points in the internal chain of relationships Supplier/ Producer Customer	Determines the internal customer's requirements and satisfaction, and pinpoints opportunities for improving internal satisfaction
INTERNAL CHAIN OF EVENTS FLOW CHART	Within the internal supplier and/or producer's processes	Identifies the steps and tasks in the internal supplier or producer's process, creating a road map for improving the internal customer's satisfaction
CAUSE AND EFFECT DIAGRAM	In the analysis of the supplier and/or producer's processes, after a clear "map" (flow chart) of the process has been created	It serves to identify and analyze the causes of internal customer satisfaction issues

The three tools above fall into a natural sequence.

⇨ The Internal Customer Satisfaction Questionnaire uncovers clues to the sources of dissatisfaction.

⇨ The flow chart is used to create a picture of what happens before the internal customer receives products or services.

⇨ Then the Cause and Effect Diagram is used to tie the two together—internal customer satisfaction issues and supplier/producer processes.

Let's take a look at how these tools work.

Internal Customer Satisfaction Questionnaire

The same methods used for determining external customer requirements can be applied to determining internal customer requirements. However, there are a few issues to keep in mind as you go through the steps that are specific to internal customers.

STEP	ISSUES SPECIFIC TO INTERNAL CUSTOMER SATISFACTION QUESTIONNAIRES
1. Identify your internal customers' requirement areas	Don't assume you know your internal customers' requirement areas. Clarify the requirement areas first, before developing your questionnaire. Take a few minutes to discuss and confirm your hunches with your internal customer.
2. Determine your surveying methodology	The ideal method is face-to-face interviewing, but if that isn't possible, use a method that will provide you with the information you need. Make sure your internal customer knows exactly what you are doing and why you are doing it.
3. Develop survey/interview questions	The same level of attention that goes into developing a questionnaire for external customers should be used for internal customers. The quality of your data depends on the quality of the questionnaire. *(See the Appendix for tips on developing questionnaires and for sample internal customer satisfaction questions).*
4. Survey/ interview your customers	Your internal customers may not be used to being interviewed as customers, so remind them of their right and obligation to let you *(their internal supplier)* know what they think. *(See the Appendix for tips on interviewing internal customers).*

In addition to using your questionnaire to check your internal customers' satisfaction with your product or service, use the opportunity to obtain general information. Questions to ask include:

✓ What products and services do you need from our department?

✓ How will we know when we have fully satisfied your requirements?

✓ How will we know when we have not fully satisfied your requirements?

✓ Is there anything that we are providing now that you no longer need from us?

Using questionnaires internally opens up lines of communication between members of your chain, which goes a long way toward improving relationships and thus customer satisfaction.

At ZampleCo, . . .

Monique, the manager of the Material Production Department, interviewed Brenda, the manager of Assembly, to get to the bottom of the dissatisfaction uncovered at that internal link. When they got to the area of suitability and preparedness of parts for final assembly, a few issues came up.

The Assembly department sometimes had difficulties mounting the latching mechanisms and were not entirely satisfied with the parts they had to work with, which came from Material Production. It seems the assembly group had felt this way for some time, but when it had raised the issue before, it wasn't taken seriously. But now that it was connected to the external customer satisfaction issue, it was a different story. Monique agreed with Brenda that the Material Production Group would look carefully at its work flow to see where the issues appeared. They decided that a flow chart would be the next step in the analysis process . . . .

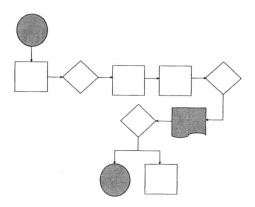

Internal Chain Of Events Flow Chart

Once a critical link has been located and the internal supplier and customer at that link have had a chance to communicate satisfaction issues in their relationship, the next step is to create a picture of what is affecting the relationship. Often the Internal Customer Satisfaction Questionnaire points to issues taking place *(or not taking place)* in the internal supplier's area. Creating a flow chart of the supplier's work flow leading to the critical link will help you find the problem area.

Note: The Appendix contains a section on creating a flow chart.

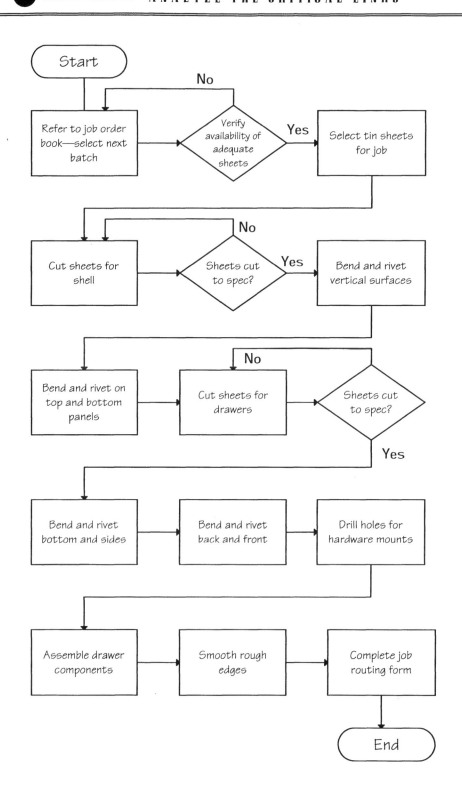

Flow chart of ZampleCo's Material Production process

Monique brought together three members . . .

of the Material Production group and briefed them on the organization's goal of improving external customer satisfaction by focusing on internal customer satisfaction. She explained the issues raised in the interview with Assembly. She wanted the group members to take a look at their work flow leading to the product they provided for Assembly, to see how they could make Assembly a more satisfied customer. Tasks were listed for creating the product they provided for the Assembly Group, and then the team converted this list into a flow chart. The group agreed to present the flow chart at the regular department meeting the next day. That way the team could get input from the rest of the department and let them know what the next step would be—to analyze the actual causes of dissatisfaction . . . .

Cause And Effect Diagram

The Cause and Effect Diagram forces us to look beyond the symptoms of a problem to the underlying causes. The visual nature of this diagram shows patterns and relationships among causes.

How to use the Cause and Effect Diagram:

A. Define the problem

Determine the relevant issue and write it in a box on a large sheet of paper, on the far right-hand side of the page.

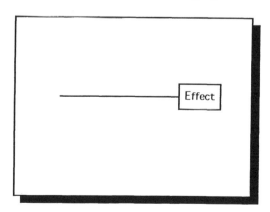

B. Define the categories for causes of the problem

Many people find it helpful to begin by using categories such as the Three M's and a P: Machines, Methods, Materials, and People; the Four P's: People, Places, Policies, Procedures; and the Four S's: Surroundings, Systems, Suppliers, Skills.

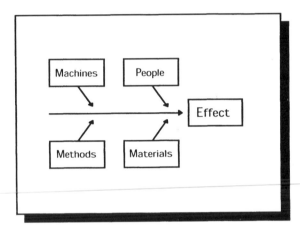

C. Brainstorm possible causes

For each of the categories, come up with as many possible contributors to the problem that you can think of.

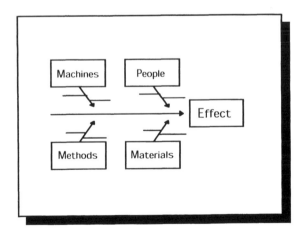

D. Identify the most likely causes

After brainstorming possible causes, narrow them down to the most likely cause.

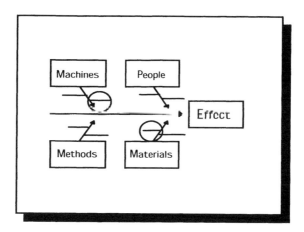

Monique brought her team . . .

together the following week, and this time included someone representing the internal customer—Larry, from Assembly. She thought it would be a good idea to have a customer's perspective on the issues. She prepared a sketch of a Cause and Effect Diagram on three adjoining sheets of flip chart paper taped to the wall.

Monique started the meeting by saying, *"The objective here is to figure out why Assembly is not completely satisfied with the product they get from us—namely, finished cabinets and drawers. I personally interviewed Brenda, their manager, and she had talked to the Assembly staff. Their main concern is that they sometimes have problems mounting the latches and locks to the drawers. Problems include the need to redrill mounting holes, rebend the surfaces, and take extra time to attach the mechanisms."*

She also added, *"Our external customers—the people who buy and use our file cabinets, are less than satisfied with the way our latches and locks work. I'm sure there is a connection between the concerns raised by both the external customer and our department's internal customer."*

With that she wrote, *"Extra work and time to mount latches and locks"* as the effect in the Cause and Effect Diagram . . . .

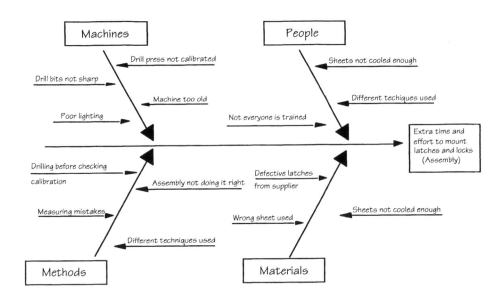

"One possible cause is working with sheets that are still warm off the roller. Since we shape them and drill mounting holes while the sheets are still warm, the tin might not be finished shrinking to its final size and shape yet," answered one of her staff. She wrote, "Sheets not cooled enough" under the Materials category in the diagram.

That got the ball rolling. Within 15 minutes the group had a list of nearly two dozen potential causes. Monique pointed out that some of these causes were showing up more than once, under different categories.

"Let's take a look at these, one by one, and see if we can narrow our list down to one or two major causes," said Monique. After another half hour of discussion, they agreed that the most important contributors to dissatisfaction were:

➨ Sheets not cooled enough, and

➨ Lack of standard method for marking and drilling mounting holes

Practice tracking down the sources of symptoms with each of the three tools we've discussed so far: Cause and Effect Diagram, Internal Chain of Events Flow Chart, and the Internal Customer Satisfaction Questionnaire.

CHAPTER SEVEN WORKSHEET:
ANALYZING THE CRITICAL LINKS

1. Who will conduct the internal customer interviews?

_____

_____

_____

2. What questions need to be asked in the interviews?

_____

_____

_____

_____

_____

_____

3. Who needs to be involved in creating the flow chart?

_____

_____

_____

_____

4. To whom will the completed flow chart be communicated?

_____

_____

_____

_____

_____

5. Who needs to be involved in creating the Cause and Effect Diagram?

_____

_____

_____

_____

_____

6. What key issues have come to the surface as contributors to external customer dissatisfaction?

_____

_____

_____

_____

_____

7. What are the specific links between internal issues and external customer satisfaction?

_____

_____

_____

_____

_____

_____

_____

_____

_____

_____

_____

_____

_____

STEP FIVE: RESOLVE CRITICAL LINK ISSUES

There are many approaches to take once the issues affecting internal customer satisfaction at the critical link are revealed. Selecting the best one for your situation will depend on factors such as the climate in your organization, the scope of the issue, cost, sense of urgency, and so on.

One approach consists of the following steps:

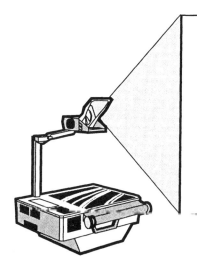

STEP 1: Establish who should be involved

STEP 2: Decide what should be done

STEP 3: Resolve the issues according to plan

Step 1: Establish Who Should Be Involved

Regardless of what approach you take, make sure the right people are involved. The issue is rarely resolved by the actions of one person. Whether a special team is formed or whether you make it a department project or a team of two, your selection should consider:

➠ Who needs to be involved to make decisions

➠ Who has the knowledge and expertise

➠ Who has to live with the outcome

➠ Who is responsible for the tasks related to the issue

➠ Who is accountable for the results

The last two points, accountability and responsibility, can be used as valuable tools in resolving satisfaction issues.

The internal customers are accountable for the product or service they receive from someone else. It then becomes theirs and they use it to create another product or service. Responsibility lies with the internal producer or supplier, and accountability lies with the person or persons on the receiving end.

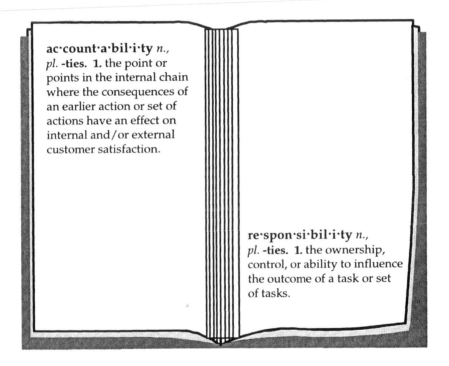

ac·count·a·bil·i·ty *n.*, *pl.* -**ties**. **1.** the point or points in the internal chain where the consequences of an earlier action or set of actions have an effect on internal and/or external customer satisfaction.

re·spon·si·bil·i·ty *n.*, *pl.* -**ties**. **1.** the ownership, control, or ability to influence the outcome of a task or set of tasks.

Using the definition of accountability above, you can see that others further down the internal chain are accountable for the consequences of something that happened several links earlier.

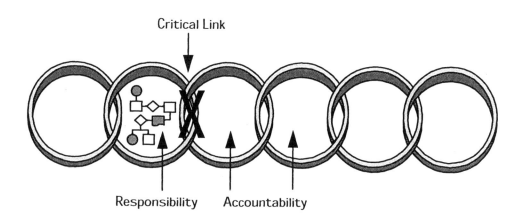

Accountability and Responsibility Matrix

The Accountability and Responsibility Matrix is a tool for defining and tracking accountability and responsibility. In this matrix, the tasks *(from the flow chart developed earlier)* are listed in the first column. These are the tasks surrounding the causes of the issues as identified by the Cause and Effect Diagram. The people responsible for the tasks are listed in the next column, and those accountable for the results are listed in subsequent columns.

Use this tool to bring together a team to resolve a given internal customer satisfaction issue. Your team will be made up of those who can control what is being done, and those who have an interest in the outcome—an ideal mix.

SPECIFIC WORK-FLOW TASKS	RESPONSIBILITY	ACCOUNTABILITY	ACCOUNTABILITY	ACCOUNTABILITY
Select sheets	Anthony, Byron	Pete (Assembly)	Angela (Assembly)	
Check sheets for adequate cool down	Anthony, Byron	Pete (Assembly)	Angela (Assembly)	
Measure and mark drill holes	Richard, Byron	Pete (Assembly)	Angela (Assembly)	Paul (Sales)

At the next meeting Monique stated . . .

that they were ready to focus on the specifics of improving their internal customer's satisfaction level. Anthony, one of the group members, responded, *"Should we figure out who is going to be part of this first? In the training program we were in last month, wasn't there a section on some sort of a matrix for deciding who should work on these kinds of things?"*

"Yes, that's right—the Accountability and Responsibility Matrix," replied Monique. *"Let's use that to put a team together."* They focused on three of the tasks from their analysis of the flow chart and the Cause and Effect Diagram. They identified who was responsible for getting those tasks done and who was affected in other departments. Based on their finished matrix, they were able to recruit three additional people to resolve customer satisfaction issues . . . .

Step 2: Decide What Should Be Done

At this point you and your team will need to decide what to do, as well as who will do it, and when. In other words—you need a plan. An Action Plan is a practical and effective tool. It can be simple, breaking down major responsibilities of what needs to be done, or a complex and highly-detailed plan.

Monique and her new team decided . . .

they would focus on two key areas:

> ➡ Coming up with a process to make sure that sheets were allowed to cool enough before they were used, and
>
> ➡ Making sure the process of measuring and drilling the holes was consistent

They decided on steps they would have to take to accomplish these goals and created the following Action Plan . . . .

ACTION STEP/ACTIVITY	RESPONSIBLE PERSON/GROUP	BEGIN DATE	END DATE	ESTIMATED HOURS	COST
Make time stamps for newly rolled sheets	Anthony	10/5	10/8	3	$95
Get material preparation to use stamp	Byron, Pete	10/5	10/20	8	$160
Flow chart ideal process for measuring	Richard, Byron, Angela	10/7	10/14	6	$120
Write procedure in manual	Monique, Pete, Pamela	10/22	11/15	10	$200
Acquire new measuring equipment	Anthony	10/12	11/15	8	$160

Step 3: Resolve The Issues According To Plan

Coming up with a plan is one thing. Carrying it out is another. Implementing an Action Plan requires:

➡ Communication between those with assigned tasks and those who have a need to know

➡ A sense of commitment on the part of the team members

➡ A means of monitoring progress

➡ Flexibility to change the plan as necessary

The team of Monique, Angela, Anthony, . . .

Byron, Pamela, Pete, and Richard realized they had a six-week project on their hands and wanted to make sure everything worked according to plan.

Angela suggested they schedule regular meetings during the six-week period, adding, "But let's not meet unless it's necessary. What if we schedule 30 minutes a week to focus on exceptions—things that didn't go according to plan or other problems we need help with?"

"If we post a blank agenda on the bulletin board, each person can write in issues to be covered in the upcoming meeting. That way we can solve problems outside of the meeting," she concluded.

"Good idea," responded Monique, "and we all need to keep in touch with each other on our progress. I'll put a copy of the Action Plan on the bulletin board, too, and that way we can make notes on it as we finish our assigned tasks."

CHAPTER EIGHT WORKSHEET:
RESOLVING CRITICAL LINK ISSUES

1. Who should be on the teams that deal with the critical link issues?

_____

_____

_____

2. Who will take the lead on creating the Action Plan?

_____

_____

_____

_____

3. What tasks need to be done to resolve the issues?

_____

_____

_____

_____

_____

_____

4. Who will be responsible for each of these tasks?

_____

_____

_____

_____

_____

5. What are the starting and ending dates for these tasks?

_____

_____

_____

_____

_____

6. How much will it cost to carry out the tasks in your Action Plan?

_____

_____

_____

_____

_____

7. How will the team manage the implementation of the Action Plan?

_____

_____

_____

_____

_____

_____

_____

_____

_____

_____

_____

STEP SIX: EVALUATE CHANGES

Why Evaluate?

There is really only one way to justify the cost, time, and effort that goes into improving your organization's internal customer service atmosphere, and too make sure that the changes you have made are the right ones. Measure customer satisfaction again. If satisfaction has improved, you are on the right track.

However, we do not live in a static world, and cannot control all the variables in the relationship between changes at a specific critical link and changes in external satisfaction levels. It is possible that the changes made at the critical link are positive and are directly related to improvements in external customer satisfaction. However, that connection doesn't show because something else is affecting their overall satisfaction with your organization.

The method you use to evaluate the effects of change will depend partly on the approach used to locate the critical link.

METHOD OF LOCATING CRITICAL LINK	RESULTS OF REMEASUREMENT
1. **Measure all the links in the chain**	If you use this method, any positive effects of internal customer satisfaction improvement will be noticeable in a remeasurement of your organization's links. Increases in internal satisfaction measurements show up in the scores for a particular critical link. Comparing increases in these scores with increases in the satisfaction scores of external customers confirms the value of the changes made.
2. **Measure from the outside in**	The effects of this process are the easiest to evaluate. You simply check changes in internal relationships with each iteration further back into the organization chain. While this is the most systematic method for evaluating the effectiveness of your internal service efforts, it is also the most costly and time-consuming of the approaches. This is best used in companies with people who are assigned to improving a firm's internal processes, such as a quality or training and development manager.
3. **Have the customer pinpoint the critical links**	Find out if the external customers are more satisfied with the process now than they were the first time you interviewed them. Checking with the external customer directly to see if changes in critical links have improved levels of satisfaction is the best approach when evaluating the effectiveness of your efforts.

Starting Over From The Top

Improving external customer satisfaction by improving internal customer service relationships should be viewed as an ongoing, dynamic process. The third approach discussed above—of going back to the customers and using their satisfaction levels to determine what further actions are necessary in your internal chain—completes a loop of customer-focused change and development. The final step of checking levels of external satisfaction is also the first step in moving through this process all over again.

CHAPTER NINE WORKSHEET:
EVALUATING YOUR SUCCESS

1. Which method did you use to locate the critical links?

   ❑ Measure all the links in the chain

   ❑ Measure from the inside out

   ❑ Have the customer pinpoint the critical link

2. How will you measure the effect of your changes against external customer satisfaction?

_____

_____

_____

_____

_____

_____

_____

_____

_____

3. How does your evaluation process relate to the method you used to locate the critical links?

_____

_____

_____

_____

_____

_____

_____

_____

_____

_____

_____

CHAPTER TEN

SUMMARY

Making improvements in internal customer satisfaction levels has a profound effect on how your organization meets external customer requirements, internal morale and motivation, and, of course, the bottom line. Let's review a few key points in this guidebook:

☑ External customer satisfaction is dependent on your organization's internal customer relationships. Improving relationships between internal customers by helping them determine what it is they require from their partners will lead to increased external customer satisfaction and loyalty.

☑ External customer satisfaction is something that can be measured and used to guide improvements within your organization's processes.

☑ By using the techniques presented in this book, you can pinpoint critical internal links, assess necessary changes in order to improve service, and promote partnership among teammates along the internal customer chain.

☑ By improving critical link relationships, you can increase external customer satisfaction and long-term customer loyalty—both of which will keep your organization on a strong competitive path.

☑ Remember: Satisfy Internal Customers First!

REFERENCE MATERIALS

Sample Internal Customer Questionnaire......................**94**

Tips For Defining Internal Customer Requirements........**97**

Developing A Flow Chart **98**

SAMPLE INTERNAL CUSTOMER QUESTIONNAIRE

CUSTOMER REQUIREMENT AREA	INTERVIEW QUESTIONS	RESPONSE LOW HIGH
Timeliness	How do you rate our department in delivering our products to you on time?	1 2 3 4 5 6 7 8 9 10
	OPEN-ENDED QUESTIONS	
	How often are we late?	
	How often are we early?	
	Can you provide a specific example?	
Quantity	How satisfied are you with our department delivering the kinds of quantities that you are expecting?	1 2 3 4 5 6 7 8 9 10
	OPEN-ENDED QUESTIONS	
	How often do we deliver a short count?	
	How often do we deliver an over count?	
	Can you provide a specific example?	

CUSTOMER REQUIREMENT AREA	INTERVIEW QUESTIONS	RESPONSE LOW HIGH
Dimension	How satisfied are you with our department delivering our product within the required dimensions?	1 2 3 4 5 6 7 8 9 10
OPEN-ENDED QUESTIONS		
How often are we out of tolerances?		
What are the most common *"out of tolerance"* events?		
Can you provide a specific example?		
Cost	How satisfied are you with the cost of the product that we deliver to you?	1 2 3 4 5 6 7 8 9 10
OPEN-ENDED QUESTIONS		
Are we over budget?		
Are we under budget?		
Can you provide a specific example?		

CUSTOMER REQUIREMENT AREA	INTERVIEW QUESTIONS	RESPONSE LOW HIGH
Responsiveness	How satisfied are you with the responsiveness of our department to your requests?	1 2 3 4 5 6 7 8 9 10
OPEN-ENDED QUESTION Can you provide some specific examples?		
Follow-through	How satisfied are you with the follow-through of our department on production issues?	1 2 3 4 5 6 7 8 9 10
OPEN-ENDED QUESTIONS Can you provide some specific examples?		

Possible General Questions for Questionnaire

➠ What products and services do you need from our department?

➠ How will I know when we have fully satisfied your requirements?

➠ How will we know when we have not fully satisfied your requirements?

➠ Is there anything that we are providing now that you no longer need from us?

TIPS FOR DEFINING INTERNAL CUSTOMER REQUIREMENTS

Before meeting with your internal customer . . .

☑ Identify the best contact persons to interview and determine time requirements.

☑ Determine participants from your group and their roles.

☑ Prepare a list of key questions to ask, focusing on customer requirements and use of your outputs.

☑ Use both open- and close-ended questions. Open-ended questions require a detailed answer allowing the customer to share information freely, while close-ended questions demand more decisive answers.

While Conducting the Customer Interview . . .

☑ Ask the customer to talk in terms of *"what really happens"* in the process *(versus what should be happening)*. This identifies improvement opportunities.

☑ Inform the customer of ongoing opportunities to provide input on any work process changes affecting him/her you plan to make in the future.

☑ Do not lead the customer. Although you may have strong opinions about his/her requirements, be sure not to sell or lobby for your point of view.

DEVELOPING A FLOW CHART

The flow chart is a planning and analysis tool used to:

 ↦ **Define and analyze service, manufacturing, or assembly processes**

 ↦ **Build a step-by-step picture of the work flow for analysis, discussion, or communication purposes**

 ↦ **Define, standardize, or find areas for improvement**

Completing a flow chart consists of four major steps:

> STEP 1: Prepare for the flow charting session
>
> STEP 2: Identify major workflow tasks
>
> STEP 3: Draw the flow chart
>
> STEP 4: Analyze the flow chart

Step 1: Prepare for the flow charting session

Prior to beginning your flow charting session:

 ⟹ Create the flow chart symbol sheet with corresponding explanations.

 ⟹ Choose someone to draw the flow chart as the team identifies the steps and the appropriate symbols.

Note: You may want to use sticky notes to help create the visual flow chart since changes may need to be made during the creation process.

Flow chart symbols

SYMBOL	NAME	EXPLANATION
	Elongated Circle	Shows the starting and ending points of a flow chart.
	Box	Any workflow task. Each box should contain a short description of the task being performed.
	Diamond	Any decision point. Each diamond should contain a question that can be answered *"yes"* or *"no."*
A	Connector	A small circle with a letter is used to connect one task of a flow chart to another.
	Document	A transfer *(or output)* of a hard copy document.
	Zigzag Arrow	Shows an electronic data transfer.
	Straight Arrow	Shows direction of process flow.

Step 2: Identify major process tasks

Begin your flow chart session by identifying the first major task in the process you've chosen to analyze *(this sets the boundary for the process)*. After this task has been identified, ask questions to stimulate thought and to expedite the completion of the flow chart.

Some possible questions include:

➠ What happens next in the process?

➠ Does a decision need to be made before the next task?

➠ What approvals are required?

Task #	Major Process Tasks	Subtasks/Decisions	Symbol
1	Receive wood block from stock	Correct size? Correct wood?	☐ ◇
2	Place into production queue		☐
3	Set up lathe for cutting	Machine ready?	☐ ◇
4	Apply holding clamps	Clamps tight?	☐ ◇
5	Get tool and cut wood block	Right cutting tool? Proper machine speed?	☐ ◇
6	Cut according to spec sheet	Wood break?	☐ ◇
7	Compare bat to spec sheet	Correct specs?	☐ ◇
8	Sign-off work order		▱
9	Forward to Finishing Dept.		☐

Example: Baseball bat company

Step 3: Draw the flow chart

Using the symbols identified in Step 1, draw the workflow tasks on flip chart paper or an overhead transparency. Every flow chart will have a start and an end *(shown by an elongated circle)*. In addition, all processes will have tasks *(shown by a box)*, and most will have decision points *(shown by a diamond)*. Decision points are yes or no questions that steer the process one way or another. Tasks may also be connected to other tasks using a connector *(shown as a small circle with a letter)*. This particular symbol is used when you need to move to another task which may be several tasks away, rather than drawing long arrow lines.

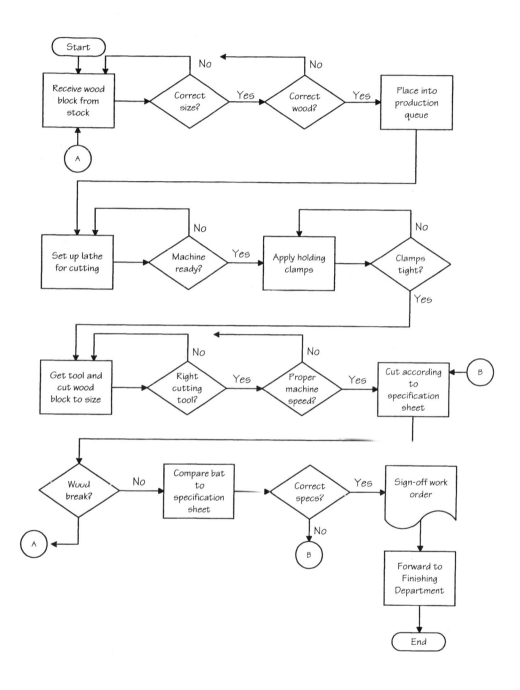

Baseball bat company flow chart

Step 4: Analyze the flow chart

The flow chart offers many opportunities for analysis including:

➤ Time-per-event *(i.e., reducing cycle time)*

➤ Process repeats *(i.e., preventing rework)*

➤ Duplication of effort *(i.e., identifying and eliminating duplicate tasks)*

➤ Unnecessary tasks *(i.e., eliminating tasks that are in the process for no apparent reason)*

➤ Value-added vs. non value-added tasks

Value-added tasks are:
Tasks within your work process that contribute to the ability to meet and/or exceed your customers' requirements. These include activities that reduce errors or tasks that decrease the cycle time of a work process, such as:

Improving processes

Making "front-line" decisions

Defining measurements

Making Action Plans

Reviewing progress

Analyzing successes and failures

Providing feedback to suppliers

Meeting with customers

Setting goals

Non value-added tasks are:
Tasks within your work process that do not contribute to the ability to meet and/or exceed your customers' requirements. These include tasks that are unnecessary or increase the cycle time of a work process such as:

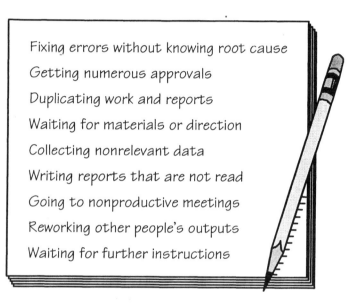

Fixing errors without knowing root cause

Getting numerous approvals

Duplicating work and reports

Waiting for materials or direction

Collecting nonrelevant data

Writing reports that are not read

Going to nonproductive meetings

Reworking other people's outputs

Waiting for further instructions

Each type of analysis listed has the potential to save individuals, departments, or companies varying amounts of time *(which translates into money)*, because a flow chart analysis will uncover any indications of loss or waste.

Before you make any process changes, though, you'll increase your analysis power if you first measure your current performance. This measurement will serve as a base line to determine if the changes you made to the process have had a positive effect.

In summary, use the Flow Chart when:

☑ You are working with a service, manufacturing, or assembly-related process. The flow chart may be more appropriate when focusing on a specific function or task and when the identification of various customers and suppliers is not crucial.

☑ You and your team need to define the tasks in a process.

☑ You are trying to determine areas for improvement in a process. The flow chart will help you and your team identify process redundancies and other problem areas.

☑ You are designing a new process. The flow chart will provide a visual representation of the process.

☑ You are standardizing an existing process. The flow chart will clarify differing viewpoints concerning the activity in a process.

PROFESSIONAL AND PERSONAL DEVELOPMENT PUBLICATIONS FROM RICHARD CHANG ASSOCIATES, INC.

Designed to support continuous learning, these highly targeted, integrated collections from Richard Chang Associates, Inc. (RCA) help individuals and organizations acquire the knowledge and skills needed to succeed in today's ever-changing workplace. Titles are available through RCA, Jossey-Bass, Inc., fine bookstores, and distributors internationally.

PRACTICAL GUIDEBOOK COLLECTION

QUALITY IMPROVEMENT SERIES

Continuous Process Improvement
Continuous Improvement Tools, Volume 1
Continuous Improvement Tools, Volume 2
Step-By-Step Problem Solving
Meetings That Work!
Improving Through Benchmarking
Succeeding As A Self-Managed Team
Measuring Organizational Improvement Impact
Process Reengineering In Action
Satisfying Internal Customers First!

MANAGEMENT SKILLS SERIES

Interviewing And Selecting High Performers
On-The-Job Orientation And Training
Coaching Through Effective Feedback
Expanding Leadership Impact
Mastering Change Management
Re-Creating Teams During Transitions
Planning Successful Employee Performance
Coaching For Peak Employee Performance
Evaluating Employee Performance

HIGH PERFORMANCE TEAM SERIES

Success Through Teamwork
Building A Dynamic Team
Measuring Team Performance
Team Decision-Making Techniques

HIGH-IMPACT TRAINING SERIES

Creating High-Impact Training
Identifying Targeted Training Needs
Mapping A Winning Training Approach
Producing High-Impact Learning Tools
Applying Successful Training Techniques
Measuring The Impact Of Training
Make Your Training Results Last

WORKPLACE DIVERSITY SERIES

Capitalizing On Workplace Diversity
Successful Staffing In A Diverse Workplace
Team Building For Diverse Work Groups
Communicating In A Diverse Workplace
Tools For Valuing Diversity

PERSONAL GROWTH AND DEVELOPMENT COLLECTION

Managing Your Career in a Changing Workplace
Unlocking Your Career Potential
Marketing Yourself and Your Career
Making Career Transitions
Memory Tips For The Forgetful

101 STUPID THINGS COLLECTION

101 Stupid Things Trainers Do To Sabotage Success
101 Stupid Things Supervisors Do To Sabotage Success
101 Stupid Things Employees Do To Sabotage Success
101 Stupid Things Salespeople Do To Sabotage Success
101 Stupid Things Business Travelers Do To Sabotage Success

About Richard Chang Associates, Inc.

Richard Chang Associates, Inc. (RCA) is a multi-disciplinary organizational performance improvement firm. Since 1987, RCA has provided private and public sector clients around the world with the experience, expertise, and resources needed to build capability in such critical areas as process improvement, management development, project management, team performance, performance measurement, and facilitator training. RCA's comprehensive package of services, products, and publications reflect the firm's commitment to practical, innovative approaches and to the achievement of significant, measurable results.

RCA Resources Optimize Organizational Performance

Consulting — Using a broad range of skills, knowledge, and tools, RCA consultants assist clients in developing and implementing a wide range of performance improvement initiatives.

Training — Practical, "real world" training programs are designed with a "take initiative" emphasis. Options include off-the-shelf programs, customized programs, and public and on-site seminars.

Curriculum And Materials Development — A cost-effective and flexible alternative to internal staffing, RCA can custom-develop and/or customize content to meet both organizational objectives and specific program needs.

Video Production — RCA's award-winning, custom video productions provide employees with information in a consistent manner that achieves lasting impact.

Publications — The comprehensive and practical collection of publications from RCA support organizational training initiatives and self-directed learning.

Packaged Programs — Designed for first-time and experienced trainers alike, these program offer comprehensive, integrated materials (including selected Practical Guidebooks) that provide wide range of flexible training options. Choose from:

- Meetings That Work! ToolPAK™
- Step-By-Step Problem Solving ToolKIT™
- Continuous Process Improvement Packaged Training Program
- Continuous Improvement Tools, Volume 1 ToolPAK™
- Continuous Improvement Tools, Volume 2 ToolPAK™
- High Involvement Teamwork™ Packaged Training Program

RICHARD
CHANG
ASSOCIATES

World Class Resources. World Class Results.^{SM}

Richard Chang Associates, Inc.

Corporate Headquarters

15265 Alton Parkway, Suite 300, Irvine, California 92618 USA

(800) 756-8096 • (949) 727-7477 • Fax: (949) 727-7007

E-Mail: info@rca4results.com • www.richardchangassociates.com

U.S. Offices in Irvine and Atlanta • Licensees and Distributors Worldwide

21216919R00069

Made in the USA
San Bernardino, CA
10 May 2015